GANGSTERS AND HOODLUMS

Iris Barry comments: "In 1912 [D. W.] Griffith found himself with plenty to say and a new ease in saying it. Social problems had not ceased to interest him; late in that year he made one of his finest short pictures, **The Muskateers of Pig Alley** with Lillian Gish and Walter Miller. A study in realism, it became an ancestor of the gangster film, decades later."

GANGSTERS and HOODLUMS

The Underworld in the Cinema

by
Raymond Lee and
B. C. Van Hecke

With a Foreword by Edward G. Robinson

CASTLE BOOKS ★ NEW YORK

This Edition Published by Arrangement
with A. S. Barnes & Co., Inc.

By Raymond Lee

Not So Dumb
Fit for the Chase
Faces of Hollywood (with Clarence Sinclair Bull)
Pearl White, The Peerless, Fearless Girl (with Manuel Weltman)
DeMille: The Man and His Pictures (with Gabe Essoe)
Gloria Swanson (with Richard M. Hudson)

Printed in the United States of America

CONTENTS

Edward G. Robinson in one of his classic poses.

FOREWORD

When Lee and Van Hecke showed me their excellent documentary on the gangster era in films, at first I felt there was little to add. Then the thought struck me that maybe they would get someone else, even an imitator to comment.

LITTLE CAESAR, many say, is the most imitated screen character in all medias. "All right, you guys, I'm boss here, See!" has been the stock and trade.

I've been parodied so many times and so broadly, that when I get to play the type of character that I've been known for, it is necessary that I do so with greater emphasis, otherwise I fall short of my imitators.

So, you readers, read and look at this record from cover to cover, see, and remember, CRIME DOESN'T PAY—unless it be in pictures.

Edward G. Robinson

GANGSTERS AND HOODLUMS

1

HOLLYWOOD'S FIRST CRIME WAVE
AND SUBSEQUENT SURGES...

As the Roaring 20s roared to their world-shaking market crash, Americans had accepted organized crime (brought on by Prohibition) as "big business," gangsters as a "Barbaric nobility," and racketeering as "a new way of life." Three headlines blacked out that complacent course: the murder of Arnold Rothstein in 1928, the '29 St. Valentine's Day massacre in Chicago, the 1931 indictment of Al Capone.

One voice from movieland, Cecil B. De Mille, spoke of things to come: "I am not a radical but now things are a question of right and wrong. The public has been milked and are growing tired of it. It is not speculation alone. There is something rotten at the core of our system. We have to get back to the simple true principles that our government was founded on."

Director Mervyn LeRoy rose to the challenge persuading First National Pictures to let him produce W. R. Burnett's best seller exposé, *Little Caesar*, starring Edward G. Robinson. Lewis Jacobs reviewed this history-making film:*

"*Little Caesar* (1931) realistically and uncompromisingly depicted the rise of an egotist through aggressiveness, ruthlessness, and organized, large-scale racketeering. It was shocking, it was hard, it was not pleasant, but it was real. Lack of sentimentality, brutal assault on the nerves with gunplay, violence, chases, tense struggles

---

* Permission to reprint granted by Harcourt, Brace & Co., New York.

over big stakes, callousness toward human feelings, appealed to a public suddenly insecure in their own lives, faced with a desperate struggle for survival and menaced from all sides.

"Despite its reformist conclusion, *Little Caesar's* condonement and even glorification of rule by force reflected the cynical state of mind, the belief in the power of force over ideals, that had taken hold in America.

"In this gangster film the audience saw the tough, fighting world where the question of right is thrust aside for the supremacy of might—that world of naked, crude essentials by which they themselves were threatened.

"Reviewed as 'the most penetrating study of the modern gangster, not very entertaining,' *Little Caesar* was an overwhelming success, making the reputation of all who worked on it and becoming the pattern for succeeding films."

The purpose of the crime movie was to expose, as De Mille had warned, "something rotten at the core of our system." The gangster cycle did this but their producers did not reckon with the strange ways of the public struggling in the depths of the Depression.

By the thousands, confused youngsters hero-worshipped the gangster, and imitated his courage-with-a-gun, his defiance of law and order no matter how great the odds. They repeated his dialogue as though it were English.

"Listen you, guys!"

"You can dish it out but you can't take it!"

"Take him for a ride!"

When James Cagney swaggered across the screen in *The Public Enemy*, they had the ultimate hero. He was virile and fearless. He was a kid who talked and acted like a man. He mussed up the big boys. He took over. He manhandled women. And he immortalized Mae Clarke's face, mashing it with half a grapefruit.

Writing in *Hound & Horn*, Lincoln Kirstein praises Cagney:

"No one expressed more clearly in terms of pictorial action the delights of violence, the overtones of semi-conscious sadism, the tendency towards destruction, toward anarchy, which is the basis of American sex-appeal."

The climax of *The Public Enemy* has never been topped for

brutal and bludgeoning shock as Cagney is crossed-fired in a gang war. His mother answers the door bell. As she opens the door his bandaged corpse falls at her feet . . .

Spencer Tracy, in *Quick Millions*, further enhanced the hero-worship with a likeable guy who said: "I'm too nervous to steal and too lazy to work."

And with that inimitable Tracy grin, he added: "But a smart guy can get away with anything if he's got brains. And I got 'em. I get the other jerks to work for me and I apply legitimate business methods to organizing crime. And if there's any lead thrown around —they get it—not me."

Columnists and clergymen spoke out against this lawless code. The public began to awaken from its trance of terror. But not until *Scarface,* starring Paul Muni with George Raft, was the gangster film forced to stand judgment in the court of censorship.

Directed by Howard Hawks and produced by United Artists, *Scarface* was the gangster picture to end all gangster pictures. Realism broke all bounds. Never had the cinema screen been ripped by such violence and bloodshed: The St. Valentine's Day slaughter, the siege of "Two Gun" Crowley by law enforcement officers, the murder of "Legs" Diamond while he lay helpless in a hospital, and dominating every foot of film—the life of power-drunk Capone.

Like most crime pictures before it this one carried this prelude:

"Every event shown in this film is based on actual experience. All the characters are portraits of actual persons, living or dead." To assuage the rising cry for censorship this was added:

"This is an indictment against gang rule in America and the careless indifference of the government. What are you going to do about it? . . ."

Richard Griffith and Arthur Mayer summed up the quick death of the bootleg-racketeer epics in *The Movies.**

"In 1931 the gangster film dominated the movies. By the middle of the next year it had entirely vanished from the screen, though not because of any lessened popularity. It was suppressed.

"The sensitive litmus paper, Will Hays, turned blue with alarm

---

* Permission to reprint granted by Simon & Schuster, New York.

at the torrents of protest which the gangster pictures evoked from the Daughters of the American Revolution, the American Legion, and that greater legion of women's and business clubs which run the machinery of community life in the United States.

"It was useless for Mr. Hays to reply that the gangster films moralized against crime and were grim object lessons that it did not pay. The small-town civic leaders knew, that Edward G. Robinson in the title role of *Little Caesar*, had become an ideal for emulation by hordes of young hero-worshippers. Nor did it help that one of the purposes of gangster films was to arouse the public to a consciousness of the prevalence of wrongdoing. There was in these topical films entirely too much evidence that existing government agencies weren't acting at all, perhaps because they were being paid off. But what probably most alarmed the respectable were certain assumptions, critical not of the breakdown of American institutions but of the institutions themselves."

With the kidnapping of the Lindbergh baby on March 1, 1932, an outraged public vented its fury. December '33 saw the repeal of the Prohibition law. The formation of the Catholic Legion of Decency in 1934 rang the death knell for the glorification of the gangster.

But like the proverbial bad penny, the gangster returned to movie screens in 1936. Producers had learned a bitter lesson. Now they showed him for what he really was—a vicious fiend preying on the weak and frightened, a madman behind bars.

Like Robinson and Cagney, one film established Humphrey Bogart as a star. Playing bestial Duke Mantee on the run in *The Petrified Forest*, Bogart put a little humanity into his killing. Leslie Howard had just signed an insurance policy over to Bette Davis. The money would send her to art school in Paris. Howard asked Bogart if he'd kill him and Bogart obliged.

As Bogie once commented on this era:

"People like a fighter. That's one of the reasons they like villains. Even when a killer is shot down at the end of a film he can still be somebody's hero."

Many major stars cut their cinema teeth on crime and gangster films. The greatest character actor of both silent and sound media, Lon Chaney, attained his first stature as a crook assimilating a cripple in *The Miracle Man*. With Priscilla Dean in *Outside the Law* he added further to his rise under the direction of **Tod** Browning, who made some of his most notable pictures.

In *The Penalty* Chaney drew rave notices for his most difficult role. Losing his legs in an accident he blames the city of San Francisco and vows to one day rule it by hook or crook. The pain and agony this dedicated man endured as a legless paranoid has never been matched by any other actor.

Chaney starred in *The Unholy Three* for both the silent and sound media and gave one of his most brilliant performances impersonating a kindly old lady. He heads a gang that includes a dumb giant and a midget, who he passes off as his grandchild. It was the last performance for the man of a thousand faces and the only one in which he spoke. His next vehicle was to have been *Dracula*.

Clark Gable copied the Cagney technique by playing a gambler, gangster and crook who roughed up his women. *A Free Soul* with Norma Shearer set his star in orbit. *The Secret Six* with Wallace Beery and *Hold Your Man* with Jean Harlow kept it rising until they crowned him—KING.

1937 saw the first tough-kid act in the sensational *Dead End*, directed by William Wyler and produced by Samuel Goldwyn, co-starring Humphrey Bogart and Joel McCrea. Six little toughs rode the movie merry-go-round to fame and fortune—Bobby Jordan, Huntz Hall, Billy Halop, Leo Gorcey, Gabriel Dell and Bernard Punsley. They were so identified with this stirring film on big city juvenile delinquency that their real names were almost forgotten. The Dead End Kids. That was it until they changed to lighter phases of breaking the law such as—*The East Side Kids*.

Not until 1942 with *This Gun for Hire* was another star born out of the killer cycle—Alan Ladd.

In the 50s such films as *The Asphalt Jungle* and *The Blackboard Jungle* showed the evils of corruption and revolt in the schools; in the latter, Sidney Poitier got his first break.

The racketeer films never regained their popularity of the 30s. But now and then a blockbuster breaks out of its old prison and rings the bell at the box-office.

Case in point. *Bonnie and Clyde*. Based on the notorious true-life killers, this sleeper blew up Hollywood like an atomic bomb. Co-starring Warren Beatty and Faye Dunaway, it reached a new high in realism. In this instance the lady was launched into overnight stardom.

As Albert Johnson summed up his reveries:*

"The legend clashed gently and movingly with the real. Arthur Penn's backward glance is filled with beauty and affection for an era, and there is so much talent involved in this film that his *Bonnie and Clyde* will remain an outstanding piece of cinema art, recreating social history in terms of today's acceptable myths.

"Above all, the mystery of Clyde Barrow and his woman accomplice remains intact. Warren Beatty has become an actor of undeniable importance with his performance here (an indelible moment, when, feeling hurt by Bonnie's sharp tongue, he stands in a field with arms raised against his chest, fists ineffectually clenched), but one still wonders about Bonnie's tattoo, and the lost notes of Clyde's saxophone, sounding old tunes in those lonely Texas nights ages ago . . ."

Will this film launch another trend?

Will the public accept violence and gunplay after the murders of so many public figures?

It is evident through its past and present that violence is an integral part of American life. Spawned on the wild west the killer instinct races through every red or blue blood. Some control it while others satiate it with murder and suicide. Killing is a pastime for some and a time saver for others who don't want to wait out a divorce decree. And still others too cowardly or respectable enjoy it as vicariously as the film fan munching popcorn, while an actor gets his guts spaghettied on celluloid.

Gabe Essoe updates the trend, "There has never been anyone to match the on-screen menace of the heavy-faced movie hood played so well by Edward G. Robinson, since he moved from Broadway stage to Hollywood in the late twenties and then went on to become the most sought after screen mobster of all time.

"Now he is back with all his cigar-biting gusto in *Never a Dull*

---

* Permission to reprint granted by Albert Johnson.

Moment, spoofing a big-time crime czar, who is planning his last big caper, the theft of a priceless museum painting."

In a recent interview with Dorothy Manners about the return of violence to the screen, Robinson commented:

"Violence as we knew it on the screen in the early '30s was an entirely different thing than it is today because society itself was different. Yes, we had shootings, and gunplay and a certain amount of horror in those old movies. But most of them had gangster themes —and gangsters mostly killed each other.

"What's more—the bad men always got their just desserts. The opening credit title on *Little Caesar* was, 'He who lives by the sword shall die by the sword!' The old hoodlum figure was either killed by another hood, or taken into custody by the hero-figure, usually a policeman or detective.

"It was part of the code of the two early film czars, Will Hays and later Eric Johnston, that crime and evil could NOT go unpunished on the screen. This applied to Westerns as well as mobster stories. No matter how well the bad cowboy was doing in the morning of the script, he was always mowed down at high noon by the good cowboy.

"This, to my way of thinking, is one of the differences between the violent films of the past and those of today. Far from emerging triumphant over evil, screen virtue today too often comes out badly trampled. The anti-hero remains unrepentant.

"*Bonnie and Clyde?*" True, they were shot to death in a few scenes at the end of their reign of terror. Meanwhile, we looked at two hours of attractive young monsters having a lot of fun robbing banks and killing people. We old movie criminals were not pretty nor particularly likeable.

"We are living in outrageous times. The country seethes with the unrest of our youth, the spinelessness of the permissive society, the toothlessness of our criminal laws, the contempt for authority. And this miserable social explosion should not be fed by the added fire of crime and violence in any or all mediums of entertainment.

"But I would like to make it quite plain that I am not in favor of any step toward congressional censorship, a possibility that has cropped up in the news lately. Censorship must come from within.

not from without the industry. And I believe it will.

"Present leaders of our business and/or art are taking a long, hard self-disciplinary look at the situation. I can assure you these men are not callous toward the enormous impact that the screen and television exert on young people.

"I tell you quite candidly that sometimes I feel a sense of guilt over my part in making violence interesting—if not attractive. My consolation is that before the final fade-out I paid for my sins by death or punishment."

Plutarch hundreds of years ago gave man wise advice when he wrote:

"Perseverance is more prevailing than violence; and many things which cannot be overcome when they are together, yield themselves up when taken little by little. . . ."

2

"EVERY EVENT SHOWN IN THIS FILM IS BASED ON ACTUAL EXPERIENCE. ALL CHARACTERS ARE PORTRAITS OF ACTUAL PERSONS, LIVING OR DEAD..."

Jean Harvey totes gun in **Guns Don't Argue,** the story of the legendary Bonnie Parker.

Burt Lancaster starred as Robert Stroud, **The Bird Man of Alcatraz.**

Mobster Al Capone was portrayed on the screen more than once. Here, Paul Muni shoots it out (**Scarface**) . . .

while Rod Steiger (**Al Capone**) gave the role a touch of elegance.

No story of Capone could be complete without the famous St. Valentine's Day Massacre. (This scene was from **Al Capone.**)

22

In **The St. Valentine's Day Massacre** Jason Robards brought a businesslike approach to the Capone role. . . .

as his henchmen planned the affair with extreme diligence.

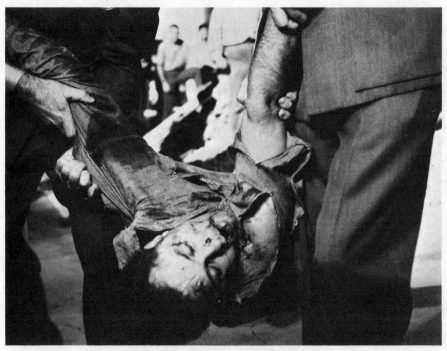

A bloody scene from **Al Capone.**

Paul Muni and George Raft in a scene from **Scarface,** with Osgood
Perkins (center) and Vince Barnett (left).

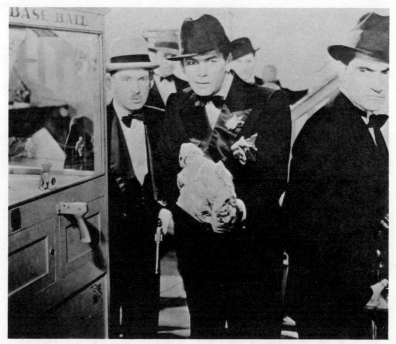

Paul Muni takes aim in **Scarface.** Vince Barnett is at left.

The St. Valentine's Day Massacre from **Scarface.**

The late Nick Adams was **Young Dillinger** . . .

Lawrence Tierney also played the infamous gangster.

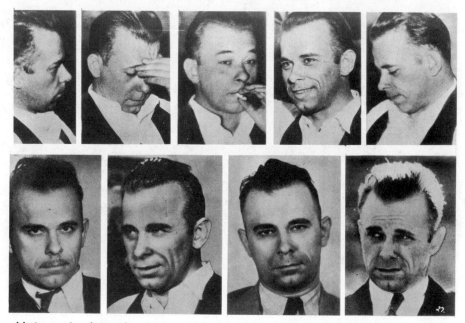

Universal released a two-reel documentary, **You Can't Get Away with It,** on the life of Dillinger. Here are nine poses of the real hoodlum.

Ray Danton played Legs Diamond in these three scenes from **Portrait of a Mobster.** Karen Steele costarred.

Robert Blake and Scott Wilson (playing Perry Smith and Richard Hickcock) break into the home of Herbert Clutter in these two scenes from **In Cold Blood.** Written and directed by Richard Brooks from the Truman Capote bestseller, the film traced the careers of the two psychopathic killers, who were eventually hanged for their murder of the entire Clutter family.

Susan Hayward played the role of Barbara Graham in Robert Wise's **I Want to Live.** Barbara Graham was sent to the gas chamber for a murder she insisted she did not commit.

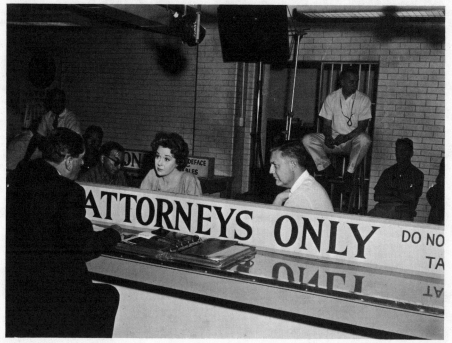

Susan Hayward in **I Want to Live.**

David Janssen as Arnold Rothstein tries to restrain an angry Mickey Rooney in this scene from **King of the Roaring Twenties.**

Veteran actor Keenan Wynn places a bet in **King of the Roaring Twenties.**

Edward G. Robinson's **Little Caesar** became the definitive Robinson role and the basis for countless imitations. Here, with George E. Stone, Robinson posed for a publicity still. This scene was not in the movie.

In this scene from **Little Caesar** Robinson threatens Douglas Fairbanks, Jr. while Glenda Farrell anxiously looks on.

In this effective scene, only the shadow of violence is seen on the screen.

35

Here, Robinson is "on the lam."

In this scene from **Little Caesar** Edward G. Robinson gives Buster Collier some gangster advice.

Edward G. and Douglas Fairbanks, Jr., in holdup scene from **Little Caesar.**

Lurene Tuttle as Ma Barker protests her innocence in this scene from **Ma Barker's Killer Brood.**

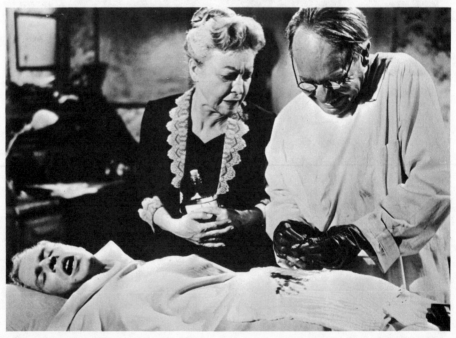

Here Lurene Tuttle looks on as an operation is performed on one of her sons.

Ma Barker wasn't afraid to shoot it out with the police.

Ma trained her sons in the fine art of armed robbery.

Screen immortals Jimmy Cagney and Jean Harlow pose with Leslie Fenton and Dorothy Gee for **The Public Enemy**, the famous story of the Prohibition era.

Cagney looks on as brother Edward Woods is gunned down.

Jimmy took time out from the violence for this tender moment with Harlow.

Here Cagney threatens speakeasy owner.

James Cagney shoves grapefruit into face of Mae Clarke in **The Public Enemy.**

42

Shootout scene from **The Public Enemy.**

Jimmy Cagney played Ruth Etting's gangster-manager in **Love Me or Leave Me.** Doris Day, in a change from her usual roles, played the part of the singer.

Robert Blake makes a forced exit in **The Purple Gang.**

Victor McLaglen, Horace MacMahon, Harry Morgan, George E. Stone, Frank Jenks, and Preston Foster line up in **Roger Touhy.**

44

Preston Foster starred as **Roger Touhy, Gangster.**

The shadow of the noose hangs over Anthony Quinn . . .

and Victor McLaglen in **Roger Touhy.**

A prison dining room scene in **Roger Touhy.**

Preston Foster and Victor McLaglen get ready for a shootout.

G-Men led by Kent Taylor finally capture Preston Foster and Victor McLaglen.

In the presence of Lois Andrews, Warden Joseph Ragen unpacks the reels of film of **Roger Touhy, Gangster** for a preview of the picture behind the walls of the prison in which Touhy was confined.

John Larch and Kathryn Grant in **The Phenix City Story**, an expose directed by Phil Karlson about America's former "City of Sin."

3

"ALL THE CHARACTERS ARE FICTITIOUS AND ANY RESEMBLANCE TO PERSONS LIVING OR DEAD IS PURELY COINCIDENTAL."

Art Lee ready to leap on then-heavyweight champion of the world, Jim Corbett, in early serial he starred in while king of the ring.

A scene from John Huston's **The Asphalt Jungle** featuring Sterling Hayden, Anthony Caruso, and Sam Jaffe.

Clark Gable cast as a gambler in **Any Number Can Play.**

Frightened Thomas Mitchell poses in front of a shadow of the Devil in **Alias Nick Beal.**

Lon Chaney is about to commit arson in **The Big City.**

A concerned Lee Marvin is being restrained as Gloria Grahame is attended to in Fritz Lang's **The Big Heat.**

Glenn Ford does battle with Lee Marvin in **The Big Heat.**

Escaped convict Edward G. Robinson shows one and all that he means business in **Black Tuesday.**

Fay Wray wasn't always being chased by a gorilla. Here she is receiving the attentions of George Raft in Raoul Walsh's **The Bowery.**

The two greatest gangsters in **A Bullet for Joy.**

John Garfield and Wallace Ford in **The Breaking Point.**

Edward G. plays it cool as gamblers Steve McQueen and Karl Malden have a dispute in Norman Jewison's **The Cincinnati Kid**—a contemporary film with a 1930s setting.

58

Author-director Elia Kazan made a few appearances as an actor, as in this scene from **City for Conquest.** Left to right: Frank McHugh, Kazan, and, of course, Jimmy Cagney.

In this scene from **City for Conquest** Cagney gets a rubdown.

Although best known for his western roles, Gary Cooper made an occasional foray into the gangster genre, as in this scene from **City Streets.**

As they did so often, Sydney Greenstreet and Humphrey Bogart appeared together in **Conflict.**

Paul Henreid and Hedy Lamarr in **The Conspirators.**

An advertisement for **Crime Wave.**

Sterling Hayden and Gene Nelson in a scene from **Crime Wave.**

Clark Gable first attracted attention as the gangster in **Dance Fools, Dance.** In this scene he appeared with Earle Fox and Joan Crawford.

Joan Crawford in scene from **The Damned Don't Cry.**

James Craig and Signe Hasso make hasty departure from the premises of Edmund Gwenn in **Dangerous Partners.**

Tony Curtis and Sidney Poitier played escaped convicts in Stanley Kramer's **The Defiant Ones.**

William Wyler's **The Desperate Hours** featured brilliant performances by Humphrey Bogart as an escaped convict and Fredric March as the homeowner he holds captive. In this scene (left to right) are Bogart, Dewey Martin, Robert Middleton, March, Richard Eyer, and Martha Scott.

Middleton tries to grab Richard Eyer; March tries to aid him; Bogart lends a hand.

Bogie threatens Martha Scott.

Bogart makes sure March is unarmed.

Dewey Martin and Mary Murphy in a less violent moment.

Bogart is about to slug March, who looks as though he knows it.

Bogart keeps anxious eye out for the arrival of unexpected guests—
like the police.

Betty Compson and George Bancroft in domestic scene from **Docks of New York.**

While detectives Arthur Gardner and Harlan Warde listen in, gangster Adam Williams sings to Edward G. Robinson (cast in the role of a detective for a change) in **Vice Squad.**

Clark Gable, in early gangster role, in **Finger Points,** with Richard Barthelmess.

James Cagney and Stuart Holmes in a scene from **Each Dawn I Die.**

Fred MacMurray and Barbara Stanwyck in famous supermarket scene
from Billy Wilder's **Double Indemnity.**

Stanwyck, Tom Powers, MacMurray, Robinson share a tense moment.

Stanwyck and MacMurray appear frightened.

Edward G. and MacMurray in office scene.

Fred MacMurray was featured in this gas-chamber scene from **Double Indemnity.** It was cut from the actual film.

Anne Francis and Key Medford talk things over in **Girl of the Night.**

Barton MacLane appears anything but gentle in **The Gentle Gangster.**

Dorothy Malone chauffeurs a determined looking Zachary Scott in **Flaxy Martin.**

Elisha Cook, Jr. threatens Scott and Malone.

Scar-faced Barry Sullivan and Joan Loring in **The Gangster.**

David Brian, in **The Great Jewel Robbery,** being ministered to by
Marjorie Reynolds.

77

Advertisement for **The Great Jewel Robbery.**

Straw-hatted, gun-toting Sheldon Leonard (now a TV producer who appears occasionally in his own productions) waits for action while Dan Seymour looks on in the background.

Richard Widmark inspects some money while Dale Robertson waits patiently by in **O. Henry's Full House,** an anthology of five of the famous author's surprise-ending yarns.

Barton MacLane holds gun on Bogart, cast as gangster Roy Earle in Raoul Walsh's classic, **High Sierra.**

Robert Taylor in tight spot in **High Wall.**

Clark Gable gets tough as Harlow watches in **Hold Your Man.**

Robert Alda on the run in **Homicide.**

June Havoc conspires with Dan Seymour (left) and Marvin Miller in **Intrigue.**

George Raft delivers warning to Havoc and Seymour.

This is a strange spot for a clergyman, but Don Murray is **The Hoodlum Priest.**

William Holden, George Raft, and Bogie as they appeared in **Invisible Stripes.**

Dick Powell leans casually against a wall as he accosts a frightened Nina Foch in **Johnny O'Clock.**

Here, Powell supplies a light for John Kellog.

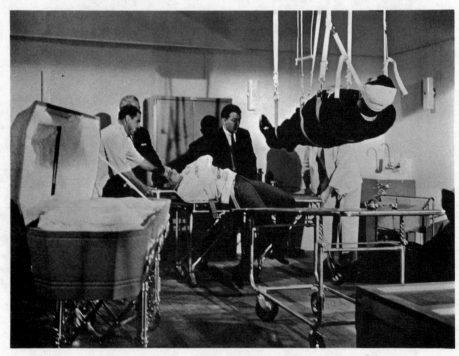

A trio of New York gangsters prepare to torture Henry Silva as **Johnny Cool** as he stares at the body of another of their enemies.

Dan Duryea and Shelley Winters seem to be sharing a secret in **Johnny Stool Pigeon.**

The picture was called **The Killers,** but lovely Angie Dickinson was in so many tight spots the film might well have been called "The Perils of Angie." Here she is securing some walking-around money with the aid of The Governor.

Angie's on the run here. Like a lady, however, she hasn't abandoned her purse.

Clu Gulager wouldn't hesitate to toss Miss Dickinson out the window. She is not even being extended the feminine privilege of screaming.

The death of John Cassavetes in **The Killers.**

One of **The Killers** was Lee Marvin.

An earlier version of **The Killers** featured Burt Lancaster and Ava Gardner.

Wendell Corey is a mild-mannered looking killer in **The Killer Is Loose.**

Edward G. tries to make things perfectly clear in this scene from **The Last Gangster.**

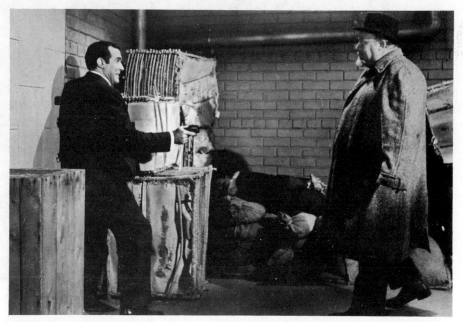

Burl Ives approaches gun-toting Ricardo Montalban in **Let No Man Write My Epitaph.**

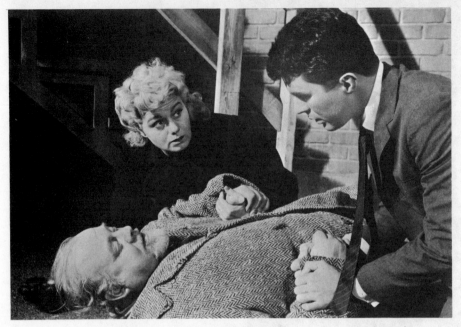

Shelley Winters and James Darren come to Ives's aid.

Mickey Rooney aims gun at guard Leon Janney in **The Last Mile.**

The Last Will of Dr. Mabuse with Klein Rogge was one of Fritz Lang's series of silent classics about master criminal Dr. Mabuse.

Peter Lorre as child-murderer in Fritz Lang's suspense masterpiece, **M** (1931).

Scenes from **The Lincoln Highwayman,** an old silent, starring William Russell.

From **The Lincoln Highwayman**.

Alison Skipworth (center) starred in **Madame Racketeer.**

97

Akim Tamiroff, Lloyd Nolan, and Mary Boland were featured in **The Magnificent Fraud.**

Greenstreet and Lorre in **The Mask of Dimitrios.** The two great stars often appeared together.

98

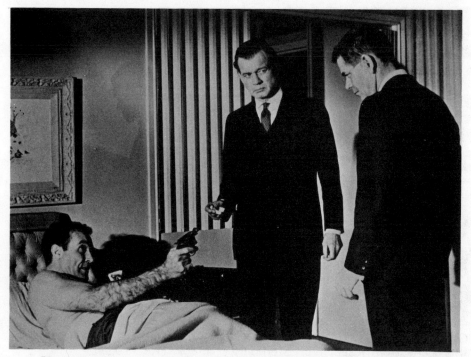

Glenn Ford is threatened by Ricardo Montalban while Joseph Cotten looks on. Ford and Montalban were cast as money-hungry detectives who attempt to rob Cotten, who played a doctor in **The Money Trap.**

Dane Clark looks prayerful in this scene from **Moonrise.**

George Bancroft, Evelyne Brent, and Clive Brook huddle together in this scene from Joseph Von Sternberg's **Underworld** (1927).

One-time Tarzan Buster Crabbe donned heavier clothing and sported a moustache for his role in **Murder Goes to College.**

TV comic Henry Morgan abandoned his jokes for a serious role opposite Stuart Whitman in **Murder, Incorporated.**

In this scene from **Murder, Incorporated** Simon Oakland, Whitman, and Morgan (left to right) go for a ride.

An assassination scene from **Murder, Incorporated.**

Whitman is being restrained by the police.

Simon Oakland gives victim an unscheduled bath . . .

now he's ready to talk.

Peter Falk was also featured in **Murder, Incorporated.** Here he tries to relax with the Sunday comic page while being kept under guard.

An advertisement for **The Murder Mob.**

The Murder Mob plays an outdoor game.

Peter Lorre learns from his mirror that he has an armed visitor, Victor McLaglen, in this scene from **Nancy Steele Is Missing.**

107

In **New York Confidential** Marilyn Maxwell divided her time between Crawford

. . . and Richard Conte.

Broderick Crawford talks tough despite his injury in **New York Confidential.**

John Drew Barrymore (left) is attacked by R. G. Armstrong in this scene from **Never Love a Stranger.**

Peter Lawford, Dean Martin, Frank Sinatra, and Sammy Davis, Jr., made modern-day spoof, **Ocean's 11**, at the time of the much-publicized "Clan."

Lawford and Sinatra look on in the background as Richard Conte suffers what proves to be a fatal heart attack, thus throwing a crimp in Sinatra's plans to rob Las Vegas.

111

Mickey Knox corners Richard Basehart in **Outside the Wall.**

Lon Chaney played hate-filled crook in **The Penalty.**

Lee J. Cobb, cast as gangster boss, turns on Aaron Saxon in **Party Girl.**

Role of gangster Duke Mantee in **The Petrified Forest** (1936), directed by Archie Mayo, made a star of Bogart. In the foreground are Dick Foran, Leslie Howard, and Bette Davis.

A burning car was always a surefire gangster prop. Here an ancient vehicle goes up in flames in **Portrait of a Mobster.**

Steve Cochran and Howard Duff uncover loot in **Private Hell 36.**

Genevieve Tobin was the **Queen of Crime.**

Spencer Tracy's career started in gangster films like **Quick Millions,** directed by Roland Brown in 1931.

Lewis Milestone directed Thomas Meighan in this rare scene from **The Racket.**

116

Robert Taylor is the good guy, Vince Edwards the hood, in these two scenes from **Rogue Cop.**

Dennis O'Keefe shares some difficulties with Marsha Hunt (center) and Claire Trevor in **Raw Deal.**

Raw Deal.

"Drive," says Bogart. Cagney won't argue (**The Roaring Twenties**).

Humphrey Bogart is surrounded by people not friendly to his cause in **San Quentin.**

Ray Milland was **The Safecracker.**

James Craig threatens radio operator in **Seven Miles from Alcatraz.**

Gable makes some inquiries in **San Francisco.**

Gable is frisked by Jack Holt (right) while Harold Huber looks on.

The old smoke in the face trick, as delivered to Joan Bennett by Dan
Duryea in **Scarlet Street**.

Dan Duryea looks like he has all the time in the world as he waits for Joan Bennett in **Scarlet Street.**

Robinson poses for **Scarlet Street.**

Edward G. about to commit murder in **Scarlet Street.**

With Robinson and Cagney, you know it's a gangster film, despite the cheerfulness of these scenes from **Smart Money.** Robinson played a gambling barber.

Nick the Barber (Edward G. Robinson) brazenly shows the card sharps a thing or two in their own line.

James Cagney and Edward G. Robinson spoofed the gangster genre in this scene from **Smart Money.**

1930's **Soldier's Plaything** was an offbeat gangster film. Dick Cramer is at the extreme left, Frank Campeau sports the derby. Ben Lyon is also featured.

John Mack Brown's Western roles came later. Here he is in **The Secret Six**, with Jean Harlow.

Peter Lorre menaces Margaret Tallichet in **Stranger on the Third Floor.**

Lawrence Tierney is a formally dressed killer in **Shakedown.**

Russell Wade is ready to **Shoot to Kill.**

Advertisement for **The System.**

Bogie and Raft were the good-guy brothers in Raoul Walsh's **They Drive by Night.**

132

Ida Lupino and Alan Hale make interesting proposal to truckdriver Raft in **They Drive by Night.** Ida tried to frame George for murder, but justice triumphed.

Barbara Stanwyck and Wendell Corey are menaced in **Thelma Jordon.**

Glynis Johns and Dermot Walsh were starred in **Third Time Lucky.**

Shootout from **Third Time Lucky.**

Charles Bickford ready for action in DeMille's **This Day and Age.**

Action scene from **This Day and Age.** Harry Green is in the foreground, holding the machine gun.

135

Alan Ladd and Veronica Lake (with her hair out of her eyes) in **This Gun** for **Hire.**

Gang leader Charles McGraw removed the bullets from the guns of
henchmen Anthony Caruso and Frank Richards.

Will John Hodiak get Lloyd Nolan's gun? (**Two Smart People**).

137

Dennis O'Keefe and Mary Meade meet under lamppost in **T-Men.**

George Bancroft in **Underworld.**

Wounded Leo Carillo is attended to in **Unseen Enemy.**

Rare early 1930s appearance of Spencer Tracy and Humphrey Bogart in **Up the River,** a Fox Film.

Bloodied Lyle Bettger totes gun in **Union Station.**

Lee Marvin sticks up bank with the aid of J. Carroll Naish (left, foreground). A frightened Sylvia Sidney looks on (right, foreground) in **Violent Saturday** . . .

Here, Miss Sidney struggles with Marvin, who has both the gun and the money.

White Tie and Tails featured Dan Duryea (left) and Frank Jenks . . .

William Bendix turned up in the wrong color tie.

142

Virginia Mayo and James Cagney were starred in **White Heat,** Raoul Walsh's classic saga of a psychopathic killer.

Sylvia Sidney and Henry Fonda in another Fritz Lang crime classic,
You Only Live Once.

Hans Conried is the victim of foul play.

Edward G. tidies up while unhappy Joan Bennett looks on (**The Woman in the Window**).

Edward G. played dual role in John Ford's 1934 gangster spoof, **The Whole Town's Talking.**

145

Robinson wraps up the body of his victim (Arthur Loft) in **The Woman in the Window** . . .

He drives to the woods to conceal the evidence.

4

STONE WALLS DO NOT A PRISON MAKE NOR IRON BARS A CAGE...

The infamous Alcatraz Island prison . . .

148

And Burt Lancaster, who portrayed perhaps its most famous inmate,
"Birdman" Robert Stroud.

Rare scene from the 1931 French version of **The Big House.**

In this action from **Big House, U.S.A.,** Ralph Meeker (second from right) is being forced into the boiler door escape by Lon Chaney, Jr. Charles Bronson is entering the door while William ("the D.A.") Talman wields knife.

Wallace Beery holds off guards in prison break from George Hill's 1930 shocker, **The Big House**, produced by M. G. M. with Robert Montgomery and Chester Morris.

Wallace Beery aims carefully in **The Big House**.

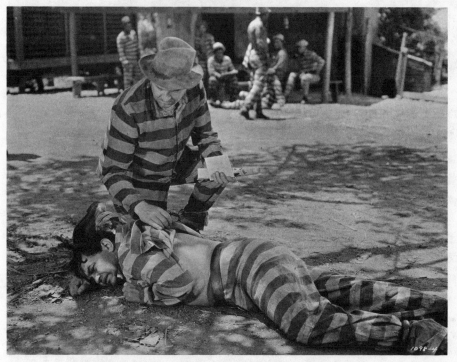

John Wray admires the quickness with which Edward G. Robinson's lash wounds have healed in **Blackmail.** Edward G. is really innocent, by the way, and shouldn't be wearing the stripes at all.

Robinson and Bob Watson hide out in swamp . . .

152

where Robinson encounters an enemy.

Charles Bickford leads prison break in **Brute Force.**

153

Eleanor Parker was nominated for an Oscar in 1950 for her role in
Caged.

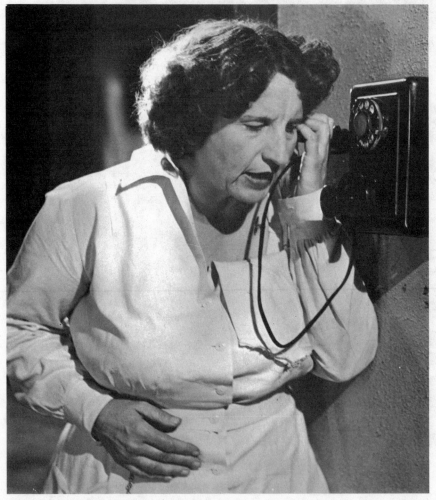

Hope Emerson was also nominated for an Oscar for her role as a guard
in **Caged.**

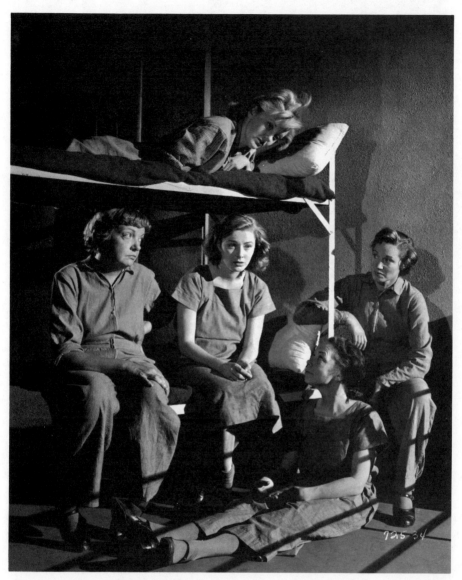

A scene from **Caged.** Seated (l. to r.) are Jane Darwell, Eleanor Parker, Ellen Corby, and Jan Sterling.

James Stewart played the part of a reporter trying to prove Richard Conte's innocence in **Call Northside 777.** Veteran director Henry Hathaway was the man in charge.

This and the following stills are from **Canon City,** a typical prison picture.

Scott Brady makes ready to ambush a guard . . .

Brady is ready to break out . . .

An example of the brutality of the guards . . .

The warden appears in the exercise yard . . .

159

Two prisoners overpower a guard . . .

Prisoners, in guards' clothing, stage an escape.

Jimmy Stewart starred in **Carbine Williams**, the story of the convict who developed a new kind of rifle while behind bars. Wendell Corey played the role of the sympathetic warden.

The girls can be tough, too, as Salley Eilers and Lee Patrick demonstrate in **Condemned Women.**

Cagney and Raft in stripes again for **Each Dawn I Die** (1939).

Fritz Lang's classic 1937 **Fury** starred Spencer Tracy, a prey to mob violence. Tracy escapes burning jail and gains vengeance on town.

162

Linda Darnell and Michael Duane are featured in this scene from
City Without Fear.

Tony Curtis chats with jailer in **The Great Imposter.**

Paul Muni's career reached its peak in 1932 with **I Am a Fugitive From a Chain Gang,** a true story directed by Mervyn LeRoy.

Hoodlum Priest Don Murray confers with one of his parishioners.

Steve Cochran terrorizes guard in **Inside the Walls of Folsom Prison.**

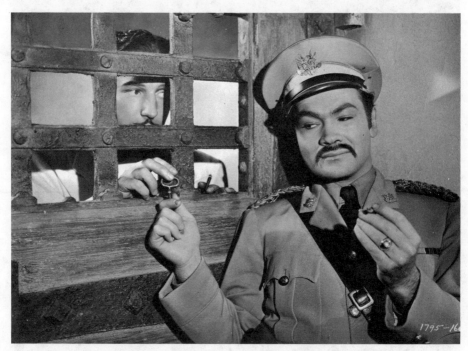

The easy way out: bribe a guard. (**The Magnificent Fraud.**)

166

Audrey Totter pays a visit to Robert Taylor in **High Wall.**

167

Gilbert Roland and Marshall Thompson confer with Harry Morgan (center) in Stanley Kramer's **My Six Convicts.**

Cyd Charisse pleads with Robert Taylor to "sing" to the D.A. in this scene from **Party Girl.**

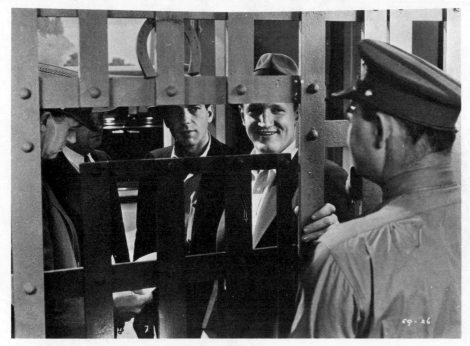

Bogie ready to enter **San Quentin.**

Bogart exchanges a few words with Barton MacLane.

169

The electric chair dominates this scene from **Stranger on the Third Floor.**

Franchot Tone is unhappy with his dinner; Horace MacMahon looks somewhat more philosophical in **They Gave Him a Gun.**

Charles Bickford and Owen Davis, Jr. confer in **Thou Shalt Not Kill.**

Noah Beery, Jr. and Larry Blake were featured in **Trouble at Midnight.**

Arthur Byron, Bette Davis, Spencer Tracy in **20,000 Years in Sing Sing,** directed by Michael Curtiz.

A scene from **Within these Walls.**

Mary Anderson and Edward Ryan seem to be very friendly in **Within these Walls** . . .

But here she seems perfectly content in the arms of Mark Stevens.

A concerned Thomas Mitchell is obviously disturbed by the gun in the hands of the inmate.

Mitchell, saddened, turns over revolver to the guard after having shot Edward Ryan. Miss Anderson has come back to him . . . too late.

Ellen Drew and Judith Barrett strike a blow for feminine equality
(**Women Without Names**).

Vice Squad saw Edward G. Robinson in the unfamiliar role of a detective. Here, he goes behind bars to attempt to crack the alibi of gangster Adam Williams, suspected of a cop-killing.

Many stars had their pictures taken behind bars. Following are just a few of the movie convicts . . .

Jimmy Cagney

Victor McLaglen

Edward G. Robinson

George Raft

Ellen Drew, Judith Barrett, Fay Helm, Louise Beavers

Sylvia Sidney and Henry Fonda

Michael O'Shea

Mickey Rooney

Ann Shirley

Barbara Stanwyck

5

YOUTH AGAINST TIME AND AGE...

James Cagney and the Dead End kids in **Angels with Dirty Faces,**
directed by Michael Curtiz (1938).

183

James Cagney threatens Pat O'Brien in **Angels With Dirty Faces.**

Wayward girls in **Are These Our Parents?**

Sidney Poitier and Glenn Ford in classic, **The Blackboard Jungle.**

A scene from **Boy Slaves.**

The East Side Kids were starred in **Boys of the City.**

An attempted theft in **The Choppers.**

186

Lita Baron tries to attend to the wounds of John Saxon in **Cry Tough.**

An advertisement for **Bowery Boy.**

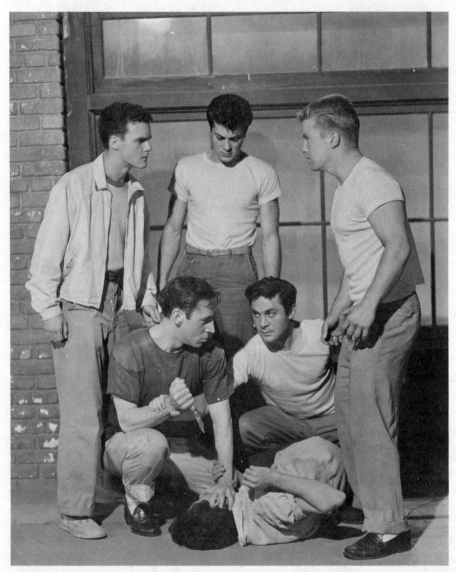

Peter Fernandez, Tony Curtis, Richard Jaekel, Joshua Shelley, and Mickey Knox were featured in **City Across the River.**

Dead End kids in **Dead End.**

Humphrey Bogart and kids in **Dead End.**

Sal Mineo confronts his enemies in **Dino.**

Two murder suspects, captured by juvenile sleuths, eye each other with mutual suspicion. Left to right, Jack Grimes, Vince Barnett, Rocco Lanzo, and Francis McDonald. The film was entitled **Fairy Tale Murder.**

190

A very young Mickey Rooney appeared with Tom Brown in **Fast Companions.**

A young Ronald Reagan was featured in **Girls on Probation.**

191

Keir Dullea played a young man accused of murder opposite Don Murray in **Hoodlum Priest.**

Murray visits a crap game . . .

Tries to persuade Dullea to surrender . . .

193

And tries to comfort him at his execution.

Johnny Nash tells gang leader Dennis Hopper that their hideout is surrounded by the police in **Key Witness.** Corey Allen, Susan Harrison, and Joby Baker are onlookers.

Dennis Hopper as he appeared in **Key Witness.**

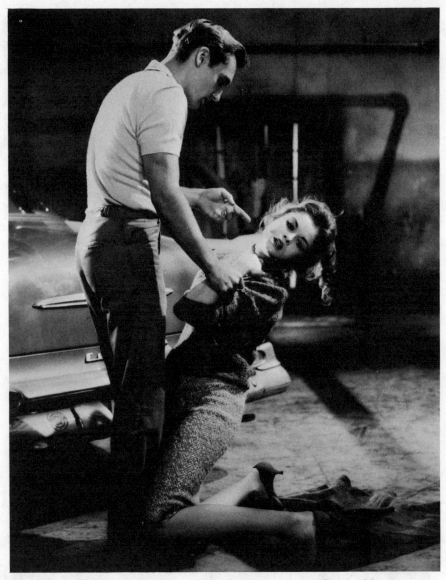

A violent argument between Dennis Hopper and Susan Harrison in **Key Witness.**

Here, Hopper pays off stolen-car money to Johnny Nash, Joby Baker, and Corey Allen.

Bogart played unusual (for him) role of defense attorney in **Knock on Any Door.** Here, he confronts John Derek in witness chair.

Sheldon Leonard confronts youthful adversaries in **Open Secret.**

Natalie Wood confronts Edward Platt in **Rebel Without a Cause.**

Director Nicholas Ray struck gold when he cast James Dean as the star of **Rebel Without a Cause.** Here are two of the scenes the late actor was featured in.

Sal Mineo in violence-filled scene in **Rebel Without a Cause.**

John Derek as he appeared in **Run for Cover.**

Gloria Jean was the star of **River Gang.**

Gloria with Jack Grimes and Mendy Koenig.

Carroll Baker gets police escort home in **Something Wild,** which was shot on location in New York City.

In this scene from **Somebody Up There Likes Me,** Paul Newman as Rocky Graziano mixes it up with the owner of the car while Steve McQueen and an accomplice steal the unfortunate victim's tires.

Newman lounging around in another scene . . .

while here he talks to some young friends.

Pierre Blanchar starred in **They Are Not Angels.**

Action centers around a modified Model T in these two scenes from
Teen Age Thunder.

Oscar-winning **West Side Story** was director Robert Wise's inter-
pretation of the famous Broadway musical derived from Shakespeare's
Romeo and Juliet. Choreographer Jerome Robbins also had much to
do with the film's success. And the music by famed maestro Leonard
Bernstein was also memorable. Set in New York in the mid-1950s,
the story dealt with two rival gangs of juvenile delinquents and a
thwarted love affair. Seen here is George Chakiris, one of the stars,
in a typical 1950s outfit.

Rita Moreno cavorts in this scene.

Violence is about to break out. Russ Tamblyn looks ready.

Richard Beymer and Russ Tamblyn struggle.

Russ Tamblyn and his gang are ready for anything.

A comic moment as Tamblyn uses garbage can for a seat.

Ward Bond (center) and Frankie Darro (right) in William Wellman's 1933 **Wild Boys of the Road.**

This gigantic scene from **Trial** is dominated by the poster of Angel Chavez, played by Rafael Sampos. Katy Jurado is seated in the front row, far left; Glenn Ford sits directly to the left of the empty seat. The orator is Arthur Kennedy.

George Hamilton played a punk in **Two Weeks in Another Town.**

James MacArthur (left) and Jeff Silver are resentful of the gentleman who asks them to take their feet down in **The Young Stranger.**

The Wild One was the first—and many feel still the best—of the motorcycle pictures. Here is Marlon Brando, leading the motorcycle gang, in the 1954 film.

213

Bearded Lee Marvin tumbles from his "bike" . . .

But he still has something to say to Brando.

6
HOODS DOWN THROUGH THE YEARS . . .

Edward Arnold and Robert Montgomery

John Barrymore and his victim.

William Bendix and Kirk Douglas in **Detective Story.**

Lyle Bettger in **Union Station**.

Charles Bickford and Burt Lancaster in **Brute Force.**

Raymond Burr in **Pitfall.**

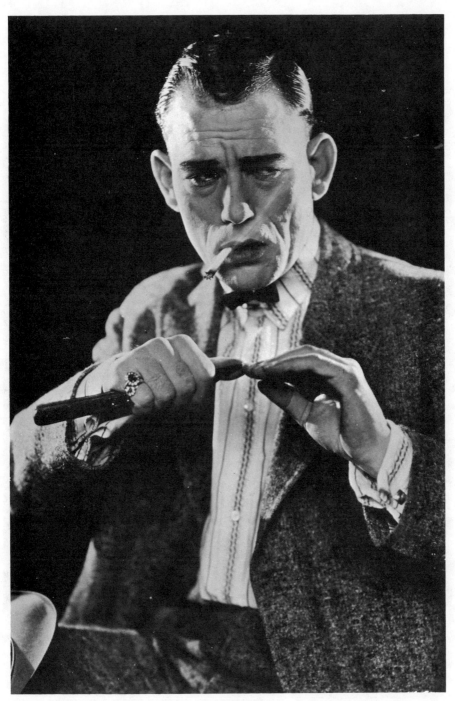

Lon Chaney

Humphrey Bogart in **San Quentin.**

Jimmy Cagney

Humphrey Bogart in classic gangster pose.

Dan Duryea

222

Clark Gable in **Sporting Blood.**

John Garfield

Peter Lorre, Sydney Greenstreet, and Joan Lorring (**The Verdict**)

Lee Marvin

Ida Lupino and Steve Cochran

Ralph Ince

Susan Hayward in **I Want to Live.**

Alan Ladd

Jack Lambert

Gene Kelly

James Mason

Mike Mazurki

Ray Milland

John McIntire

233

A young Paul Muni

Maureen O'Hara and John Garfield in **Fallen Sparrow.**

Jack Palance

236

Kirk Douglas and Eleanor Parker in **Detective Story.**

George Raft

237

Jason Robards as Al Capone.

Rod Steiger

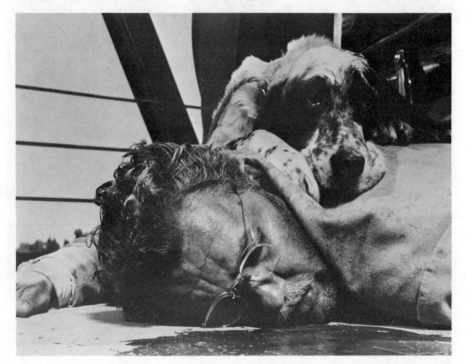

Edward G. Robinson

Robert Taylor

Lawrence Tierney and Anne Jeffreys

Spencer Tracy

245

Natalie Wood with George Chakiris in **West Side Story.**

7
CRIME ALSO HAS A BELLY LAUGH

There is nothing funny about being shot in the belly, but when it's done by Laurel and Hardy, Abbott and Costello or with Chaplin using a brick instead of a bullet, it's a riot. And the screen comics poking movie fan ribs around the world on every subject, no matter how sacred or controversial, didn't miss the mark, hitting high hilarity with the gangster and criminals in all areas.

Abbott and Costello run into trouble when they become murder suspects in **Abbott and Costello Meet the Killer.**

Sid Caesar discovers definite evidence of foul play (Dom DeLuise is the victim) in **The Busy Body.**

Tyler Brooke and Vernon Dent in prison setting.

Marlon Brando, Jean Simmons, Frank Sinatra, and Vivian Blaine starred in the screen version of **Guys and Dolls**, Frank Loesser's immortal musical based on characters from Damon Runyan short stories.

Lynne Overman (clean) looks very superior to Roscoe Karns (spattered) in **Partners in Crime.**

Laurel and Hardy entertain some unsavory guests . . .

here, the boys, in prison stripes, smilingly obey (?) guard's instructions.

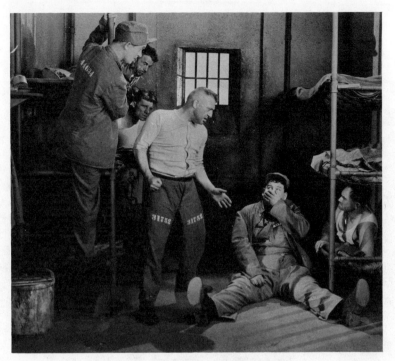

Oliver has had his nose bloodied.

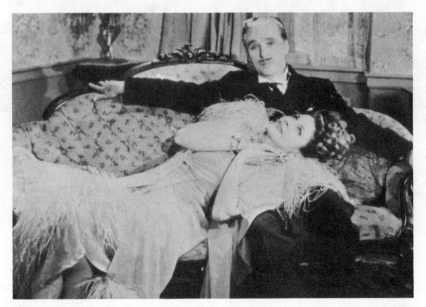

Charlie Chaplin as the wife-killer for profit in **Monsieur Verdoux**
with Martha Raye (1947).

Bob Hope cavorts in drag, Lloyd Nolan plays it straight in **The Lemon Drop Kid** . . .

Here, Lloyd shows off his argyles.

Although George Raft's gangland-style execution doesn't exactly appear to be a comic moment, it was the focal point for subsequent hilarity in Billy Wilder's famous **Some Like it Hot.**

Old-time comics Wheeler and Woolsey on the rockpile.

Arsenic and Old Lace was the classic comedy-murder-mystery. Here, Raymond Massey (with shovel) encounters Peter Lorre.

Josephine Hull and Jean Adair feed poison to unsuspecting Edward Everett Horton.

255

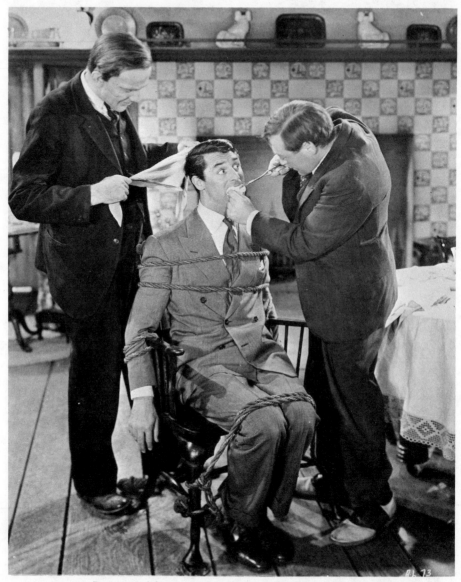

Peter and Raymond bind and gag Cary Grant.

8

EPILOGUE

They say history repeats itself. And motion pictures, through their long run of over seventy years, certainly have adhered to all manner of themes—again and again.

As the one and only Mr. Edward G. Robinson said, "crime doesn't pay—unless it be in pictures!" Recently *Bonnie and Clyde* paid off at the box-office in the millions and a few producers jumped on the violence band-wagon. Even such westerns as *The Wild Bunch*, made blood and gore hard for those with weak stomachs to sit through. But since this sensational starrer for Warren Beatty and Fay Dunaway came and went the few imitators came and went—but without benefit or profit.

Have we seen the last of the gangsters and hoodlums?

We think not. As Mr. Peter Cowie writes of *Bonnie and Clyde:**

"If, the film appears to say, life is nothing much to lose, then crime pays: it produces a peculiar intoxication that makes the world appear crass and slow-thinking . . ."

Any defense, film fan?

---

* Permission to reprint granted by A. S. Barnes & Co. from *Seventy Years of Cinema*, by Peter Cowie.

Faye Dunaway and Warren Beatty have a little target practice in director Arthur Penn's **Bonnie and Clyde.** Beatty also produced the film that many critics consider to be one of the finest of recent years.

Faye totes gun; Warren totes Faye.

Their first killing: a grocer.

Here the growing Barrow gang makes its getaway after a bank job. Michael J. Pollard, as C. W. Moss, is in the foreground. Gene Hackman, as Clyde's brother Buck, is to the left of Miss Dunaway.

Michael J. Pollard totes machine gun as he shoots it out with police . . .

two of whom fall.

Determined Beatty drives on despite bullet in the windshield. Estelle Parsons, as Clyde's sister-in-law Blanche, was hit.

Scenes from the finale, criticized by some for its excessive violence and praised by others, for its cinematic excellence. Here, the two gangsters shoot at police.

Finally caught in an ambush, Bonnie is hit . . .

So is Clyde . . .

THE END